MA'AM IN COMMAND

A Guide for Women Aspiring to Command or Chief Positions

This book is dedicated to my daughter, Erica, the strongest, most intelligent woman I know. The world is better because of you. I love you.

I want to thank Chief Gene Ellis (ret.) for writing the Foreword to this guide. I would also like to thank him for his unwavering support and for sharing this life with me. I love you.

Copyright pending

No part of this book may be reproduced, stored in a retrieval system, or transmitted in any form or by any means, electronic, mechanical, photocopying, recording, or otherwise, without the prior written permission of the author, except for brief excerpts used in reviews or scholarly articles.

Published by Amazon Kindle Direct Publishing

Cover design by Lieutenant Daniel Franklin

ISBN 9798278267119

First Edition

TABLE OF CONTENTS

Dedication	2
Forward	5
Introduction	7
Chapter 1 Complexities of the Office	14
Chapter 2 Derailers	18
Chapter 3 Building Strategic Networks	30
Chapter 4 The "It" Factor	34
Chapter 5 Skillsets Needed	48
Chapter 6 Preparing for the Process	65
Chapter 7 The Interview	70
Chapter 8 You Have an Offer, Now What?	73
Chapter 9 You Can't Win Them All: When It All Goes South	83
Chapter 10 Is this the Hill?	92
Chapter 11 Words From the Wise	93
Chapter 12 Summary	95
Chapter 13 Examples	96

FORWARD

Ma'am In Command is a must-read for anyone seeking leadership opportunities in the policing profession. I once believed I fully understood the challenges faced by female leaders in our field. The truth is, I had no idea—until I married a female police chief. Only then did I witness firsthand just how different the experience can be.

Ma'am In Command provides compelling insight into those challenges, the distinct expectations placed on women in policing, and the opportunities that can emerge despite them. More importantly, it offers readers practical tips, actionable tools, and useful templates for pursuing their goals in police leadership.

Some of the anecdotes may be surprising—perhaps even unsettling—given that they occur in the 21st century, but they are invaluable for understanding the realities and perspectives of a female leader in law enforcement. I've also heard the stories that didn't make it into the book, and they are even more astonishing.

Chief Carrie Ellis is a talented and highly effective leader. Her book is a true "how-to" guide for anyone—regardless of gender—seeking to become a police chief or to step into any leadership role within public safety. I am blessed to not only know her as "Chief" but also as the love of my life.

Chief Gene Ellis (ret)
Executive Director
Texas Police Chiefs Association

Ma'am In Command
A Guide for Women Aspiring to Command or Chief Positions

Introduction:

In law enforcement, the role of the Chief of Police stands as the pinnacle of leadership and authority within the policing structure. It is a position surrounded by immense responsibility, requiring individuals to possess not only tactical prowess and keen strategic acumen but also a profound and unwavering commitment to justice, ethical conduct, and community service. This role is often seen as a critical linchpin in fostering trust and cooperation between the police force and the communities they serve. Traditionally, the position of Chief of Police has been predominantly occupied by men, which reflects the deep-rooted gender disparities that persist within the law enforcement field. This historical trend underscores challenges that women face in ascending to such influential roles. Nationally, female chiefs are about 3.6% overall, with this number increasing to over 16% in cities with populations over 250,000. Conversely, this number drops significantly in cities with a population of 50,000 or fewer.[i] Texas is not faring as well as of this writing; only about 1.8% of police chiefs are female[ii]. This statistic starkly emphasizes the ongoing issues of gender inequality in this profession. In raw numerical terms, this means there are only about 30 female police chiefs in Texas. Such numbers reveal the significant underrepresentation of women in these critical leadership roles, highlighting the need for continued efforts to promote women to leadership and chief executive roles and to encourage more women to pursue careers in policing.

However, in light of the evolving societal landscape, it is abundantly clear that times are indeed changing. This shift is ushering in new and diverse perspectives on gender roles and leadership across various sectors. Across the globe, women are not just breaking but are shattering the longstanding glass ceilings that have previously restricted them. They are rigorously challenging entrenched norms and barriers across every imaginable field, and law enforcement is no exception. The progressive ascension of female police officers into prominent and influential leadership positions is not merely a symbolic victory in the ongoing pursuit of gender equality; instead, it stands as a powerful testament to the undeniable talent, resilience, and unwavering dedication that women consistently bring to the law enforcement profession. Some agencies and associations are taking substantial steps to promote and encourage women's roles in leadership at all levels of law enforcement agencies, thereby enhancing the overall effectiveness and diversity of these institutions, which ultimately benefits the communities they serve. However, we have not fully arrived... yet.

Numerous organizations are playing a pivotal and crucial role in this important initiative aimed at promoting gender equality within law enforcement agencies around the country. Among these organizations, the National Association of Women Law Enforcement Executives stands out prominently, as it not only wholeheartedly endorses but also actively supports and promotes the advancement of women seeking leadership positions within the law enforcement community. This association is dedicated to ensuring that women have ample opportunities to ascend to these influential roles, thereby helping to create a more balanced and representative leadership structure within the field.

In addition to national efforts being made to achieve transformative goals in law enforcement, various state-level associations are also making remarkable and significant strides in this direction, demonstrating their unwavering commitment to positive change. For instance, the Texas Police Chiefs Association, a prominent organization in the State of Texas, has recognized the vital need for change in law enforcement practices and has actively taken concrete steps to facilitate this crucial transformation. They have a dedicated committee focused on promoting, supporting, and advancing women in law enforcement executive roles throughout the State of Texas. This committee, established in 2019, not only emphasizes the importance of having diverse leadership within law enforcement but also highlights the multitude of positive impacts that such diversity can have—not just on the effectiveness and operational success of law enforcement agencies, but also on the communities they serve and protect.

The ongoing transformation currently taking place within the intricate fabric of law enforcement signifies a broader and significantly deeper commitment to promoting women in law enforcement. This commitment, in turn, is actively reshaping the very culture of law enforcement as we understand it today. By thoughtfully making these necessary adjustments and focusing intently on promoting diverse leadership, these organizations are not only changing the internal dynamics and structures within law enforcement but also setting a powerful and influential example for other fields and sectors to emulate and adopt. Ultimately, this initiative seeks to create a law enforcement environment that is not only more reflective of our diverse society as a whole but also one that enhances community relations and builds stronger, more meaningful trust between law enforcement and the public it is dedicated to serving and protecting.

This guide, titled "Ma'am in Command: A Guide for Women Aspiring to Command or Chief Positions," serves as a comprehensive and detailed roadmap specifically designed to empower and inspire women on their transformative journey towards leadership roles within law enforcement. It acts not only as a guide but also as a manifesto for significant change, passionately advocating for increased representation and promotion of women to the highest echelons of policing, where their voices and perspectives can lead to more effective law enforcement practices. Through its insightful content and practical advice, this guide seeks to equip aspiring female leaders with the tools, confidence, and strategies necessary to navigate the unique challenges they may face in a predominantly male-dominated field, thereby fostering a more balanced and diverse environment within the realm of policing.

This guide combines practical advice, inspirational stories, and expert insights to equip aspiring female leaders with the tools and knowledge they need to navigate the complex landscape of law enforcement leadership. From overcoming systemic barriers and confronting implicit biases to honing leadership skills and building strategic networks, each chapter is designed to address the unique challenges and opportunities women face in pursuing the Chief of Police position. For instance, imagine walking into your first command staff meeting and realizing you're the only woman at the table. This guide is designed to help you not only sit at that table—but **lead** it.

Drawing upon the wisdom of trailblazing women who have already achieved success in this field, this book serves as a beacon of guidance and encouragement for women at every stage of their law enforcement careers. Whether you are a rookie officer with dreams of ascending the ranks or a seasoned veteran aiming for the top, "Ma'am in Command" will arm you with the insights and inspiration you need to make your mark on the future of policing.

Chapter 1

Complexities of the Office

"...the position necessitates resilience, often referred to as having a thick skin, alongside an abundance of grit and determination."

Listening to colleagues engage in conversations about their diverse experiences as young women navigating the complexities of working in law enforcement powerfully underscores the urgent need for a well-structured resource that effectively guides and supports women who aspire to hold influential positions, such as chiefs of police. This necessity is particularly highlighted by the fact that, much like in the broader law enforcement profession, the representation of women in executive roles within law enforcement is alarmingly lower than that of their male counterparts. The women currently occupying these pivotal positions do not adequately reflect the diverse populations we are entrusted to serve, pointing to a significant gap in representation.

In smaller law enforcement agencies, this issue is even more pronounced, as women often lack female mentors within their command structure. This lack of guidance and support can hinder their career development and professional growth, leaving many without the skills and experience needed to advance to command-level positions or, ultimately, to the critical chief executive role. This does not imply that there are no mentors for women, but it does highlight the need for more women in the profession and in executive positions. The competitive nature of this field intensifies the challenges faced by women, who often feel the pressing need to stay consistently a step ahead of their male colleagues to succeed and advance in their careers. Moreover, when the educational requirement for advancing in this profession is set at a Bachelor's degree, many women actively seek to enhance their qualifications by pursuing a Master's degree. This pursuit not only increases their chances of advancement but also equips them with the knowledge and skills essential to today's evolving law enforcement landscape.

In today's rapidly evolving social landscape, the question arises: What qualities and skills are essential to becoming a successful police chief? Drawing on the author's personal experiences in the field and those of colleagues, both female and male, it can confidently be asserted that the role demands a unique blend of attributes. These include not just creativity and effective listening skills, but perhaps more importantly, an unwavering, innate desire to serve the community and its citizens. Without such a deep-rooted commitment to service, achieving lasting success in this role may prove to be elusive, at best.

Furthermore, the position necessitates resilience, often referred to as having a thick skin, alongside an abundance of grit and determination. The reality is that this profession is notorious for its challenges and demands, making it clear that the responsibilities of a Chief of Police are not suited for those who are faint of heart. Each day presents a new set of obstacles to navigate, testing the Chief's resolve, judgment, leadership skills, and resilience. However, amid these challenges lies the potential for immense rewards, as few roles offer such profound opportunities to impact lives and foster positive change within the community.

Police chiefs face daily challenges that are taxing on their physical and mental health. Chiefs are ultimately responsible for the conduct of their officers. Chiefs are accountable to the citizens they serve and to the profession. What is it about females that makes a good chief? We are not better chiefs of police than our male counterparts; we just do the job differently. Remember, 5+4=9, but so does 6+3. The same qualities that make us great Officers, Sergeants, and Lieutenants are also the same qualities that make us great as a Chief. Those are the ability to listen, de-escalate, and serve others. However, we face an obstacle that most of our male counterparts do not. As females, we must also have the ability to get out of our own way.

What does it truly mean to get out of our own way? This question is particularly relevant for women in the workplace, as we often find ourselves our own worst enemies. Internally, we often grapple with the voices of self-doubt and criticism, which can significantly undermine our success.

Chapter 2

Derailers

"…notable trend is the tendency to prioritize consensus building and harmony over assertiveness and self advocacy…"

Internal Derailers

We have been socialized to place a high value on hard work, often to the extent that we overlook the complicated and politicized nature of our professional environments. Many of us believe that performing well and doing our jobs effectively entitle us to receive promotions and recognition for our efforts. However, it is crucial to recognize that there is far more to career advancement than simply putting in long hours and producing high-quality work products.

Interpersonal skills and the ability to engage in meaningful conversations with others are equally, if not more important, to our success. This becomes particularly evident in the highly politicized environment that comes with responsibilities such as being a Chief. Within this context, the relationships we cultivate with colleagues in our office, as well as with members of the executive team and governmental leaders, are invaluable.

I recall a male colleague who made it a point to take an hour or so each day to stroll to his office. During this time, he would stop by everyone's office and engage in casual conversations for a few minutes. This was not merely idle chatter; he was intentionally building and nurturing relationships that would serve him well in his career. Those few minutes he dedicated to socializing and connecting with others gave him a distinct advantage, as he invested time in fostering bonds that would lead to mutual support.

On the flipside, women often perceive this kind of behavior as nothing more than slacking off. Too frequently, we find ourselves hunkered down at our desks, absorbed in completing the most recent tasks or projects, thus missing out on opportunities to build essential connections with our colleagues. This approach may inadvertently hinder our career progression by overlooking the critical importance of relationship-building in the workplace.

Another prevalent issue that often derails women's career progress is their tendency to downplay or downsize the significance of their own achievements and capabilities. This particular phenomenon is frequently referred to as "imposter syndrome," a term that encapsulates the feelings that many women experience, leading them to internalize profound feelings of inadequacy or self-doubt, even in the face of demonstrable accomplishments. This internal struggle can manifest in various ways, where women, rather than celebrating their successes, may find themselves minimizing their achievements or attributing them to external factors, such as luck or the help of others. Consequently, by not fully owning their wins, women may inadvertently undermine not only their own credibility but also their visibility in the workplace. This can create significant barriers, making it increasingly challenging for them to advance their careers in a professional landscape that already presents numerous obstacles.

Additionally, women may often find themselves ensnared in the challenging and sometimes overwhelming trap of perfectionism. This is characterized by a relentless striving for unrealistic standards of performance, achievement, and overall productivity. This insatiable quest for flawlessness can lead to severe consequences, including burnout, heightened anxiety, and a noticeable decline in self-confidence. These feelings arise as women continuously grapple with the immense pressure to excel in every facet of their professional and personal lives, creating a perpetual cycle of self-doubt and stress. Over time, perfectionism can evolve into a significant derailer of personal and professional progress, effectively hindering women from taking essential risks, seizing valuable opportunities, and advocating for themselves in a manner that aligns with their true potential and aspirations. It can stifle creativity and innovation, as the fear of not meeting high expectations discourages women from exploring new paths or taking on challenges that might lead to growth.

Another notable trend is the tendency to prioritize consensus-building and harmony over assertiveness and self-advocacy, particularly in the context of the workplace. This inclination can significantly hinder women's ability to adequately assert their needs and establish firm boundaries in professional settings. While it is undeniable that collaboration and effective teamwork are crucial components of a successful work environment, women may avoid conflict or confrontation, often to the detriment of their personal and professional interests. This avoidance can lead to situations in which others take undue credit for original ideas or valuable contributions, which can be disheartening and demotivating. Moreover, this reluctance to assert oneself in a variety of work-related scenarios can ultimately limit opportunities for career advancement, creating barriers that perpetuate existing gender biases. These biases tend to favor individuals who exhibit more assertive or aggressive behavior, further entrenching inequalities in workplace dynamics. Thus, it is essential to address these patterns to foster an environment that encourages all individuals, regardless of gender, to voice their perspectives and defend their contributions effectively.

Perfectionism and consensus-building are classic examples of what is commonly known as Goldilocks syndrome. If women in law enforcement are too confident and assertive, we are labeled as a bitch. If we are not assertive enough, we are not cut out for the job. If we show empathy, we are perceived as too sensitive; if we show none, we are perceived as cold and heartless. When we speak out about the disparities in law enforcement, we are labeled as complainers who cause trouble and are just making excuses, but not speaking up hurts us and ultimately the law enforcement profession.

Women often face significant challenges in achieving a work-life balance, especially in male-dominated industries, where long working hours and intense competition are not only typical but expected. This struggle is compounded by the need to balance their professional ambitions with various caregiving duties, household responsibilities, and personal interests, which can create tremendous pressure. As they navigate these demanding expectations, many women experience feelings of guilt over not being able to dedicate enough time to their families or personal lives, leading to an overwhelming sense of stress and eventual fatigue.

In summary, while women face a multitude of external challenges and obstacles in the workplace, it is equally critical to address internal derailers that may hinder their progress. These internal derailers can significantly impede their ability to unlock their full potential and ultimately advance their careers in a meaningful way. By actively recognizing and confronting these tendencies, which may include self-doubt, a relentless pursuit of perfectionism, an avoidance of conflict, challenges associated with work-life imbalance, and a lack of adequate support systems, women can take significant steps towards overcoming the barriers that stand in the way of their success. It is essential to understand that, through cultivating self-awareness, developing resilience, and implementing strategic action plans, women can effectively derail-proof their careers.

By doing so, they not only enhance their own professional journeys but also pave the way for greater gender equality and increased diversity within the workplace. Therefore, the journey towards achieving gender equality in professional settings demands both an acknowledgment of external factors and a commitment to overcoming internal obstacles.

External Derailers

It may come as a shock to some, but there are still people who have strong negative opinions about women in law enforcement. Some of these opinions are from within the profession, while others come from outside of it. Either way, they can be difficult to overcome. With assistance from the Law Enforcement Management Institute of Texas (LEMIT), this author solicited responses from female leaders in law enforcement regarding phrases they have been asked or told throughout their careers, specifically after attaining a command-level or chief position.

The responses were enlightening as they illustrated the biases plaguing the profession and impeding relationships. The responses range from "you are too feminine looking" to "you are too masculine looking." They also include statements that females are more emotional than their male counterparts or are just too emotional. Also, one respondent said she was told the other command staff members would never take her seriously. While these statements reflect biases still evident in policing, they do not encompass all members of law enforcement. It does identify opportunities for improvement, however. One colleague related a story from a job interview at a very rural agency. She dressed in standard interview clothing, a suit and heels. After her interview, but before signing a release, a member of the interview panel called one of her colleagues from a neighboring agency to ask whether he believed she had the **ability** to work patrol. He did not ask if she would be willing to work patrol; her ability was in question. This was not 5, 10, or 20 years ago; this was in 2024.

Throughout many police organizations, subtle nuances and attitudes discourage women from becoming police officers. It also discourages women from seeking supervisory, command, and executive positions. Furthermore, the insufficient availability of crucial support systems—such as flexible working arrangements that adapt to employees' needs, comprehensive parental leave policies that ensure parents can take the necessary time off without fear of repercussions, and understanding workplace cultures that prioritize inclusivity and empathy—can make it significantly more challenging for women to maintain and advance their careers over the long term. Todak (2023)[iii] states that our profession is still suffering from a glass ceiling, and statistics support this assertion. The statistics, as previously mentioned, clearly show that there are more men than women with whom to build professional relationships. Women do not have the same life experiences from which to draw, nor do we have the same perspectives.

In addition to the subtle nuances within agencies, there are some not-so-subtle clues that we have not evolved enough. When this author walks through an exhibit hall with a male colleague at a law enforcement conference, vendors seldom acknowledge the female (me) first. This is not a situation that is unique to me; one colleague walked through an exhibit hall with her husband, who is not in law enforcement, and she experienced the same treatment. Their attention is usually directed at the male first no matter what title is on the name badge. This was a topic of conversation with my now husband, and while he nodded as if he understood, I prepared him for how the vendors would behave. These interactions in the exhibit hall proved to be an eye-opening moment for him, as he gained firsthand insight into one of the unique challenges female employees in law enforcement face.

A chief known to this author had a discussion with an employee about wearing an outer vest carrier. The employee, a female, was advocating for wearing the outer vest, and he was opposed. She finally explained that the outer vest makes it easier to pump after having a baby. He was taken aback because he would never have thought of the convenience of an outer vest for this purpose.

This multifaceted combination of pressures, including societal expectations and institutional barriers, can ultimately derail professional trajectories, seriously hindering the ability to actively pursue opportunities for advancement and achieve career goals. Without a thorough and meaningful reevaluation of current workplace policies and practices, many women may continue to grapple with the difficulties of balancing their various roles effectively, which can lead to lasting and far-reaching implications not only for their professional journeys but also for their overall well-being, mental health, and quality of life as a whole. This author facilitated a discussion with colleagues, mostly male, about serving as a chief executive and fulfilling the role of wife and mother. Many spoke up and praised their spouses for all they do at home, which enables them to succeed. It was an eye-opening moment when they realized that many women serving as chiefs are largely responsible for the same household tasks as their spouses.

Additional examples include a single mother who is habitually late to work or frequently calls in sick because her child or children are ill or have doctor or dentist appointments. Also, women may be more hesitant to seek promotional opportunities because it would most likely cause them to change shifts. Often, new supervisors are put on a night shift, and childcare for an overnight shift is practically non-existent, especially in rural areas.

Ultimately, a significant lack of access to vital mentorship, effective sponsorship, and valuable networking opportunities can severely hinder women's career progression and advancement. This issue is especially pronounced in workplace environments where men predominantly dominate informal channels of support and advancement. In the absence of capable mentors or sponsors who can offer necessary guidance, robust advocacy, and meaningful career opportunities, women may struggle to navigate complex organizational politics effectively. Furthermore, they may encounter considerable challenges when attempting to break into male-dominated networks, which often serve as gateways to professional growth and opportunities. This situation can result in women being denied access to critical developmental resources that are essential not only for professional success but also for personal growth within their careers. Therefore, organizations must address these pervasive systemic barriers. Fostering a culture that emphasizes inclusion, support, and equitable access to opportunities is not just beneficial but essential for mitigating the detrimental and derailing effects of gender bias that continue to persist in the workplace today.

CHAPTER 3

BUILDING STRATEGIC NETWORKS

"Operating in a silo will never allow full potential to be reached."

Operating in a silo will never allow full potential to be reached. There is a wealth of information to be gained from informal conversations with colleagues. This can be tricky, however. Women do not get treated like men treat each other. Women typically do not receive the same level of communication as men. I refer to it as the Deer Camp Club. Whatever the reason, it is a hurdle. This author has called colleagues when they are off-duty, needing an answer to a question, and the tone of voice is, more often than not, distinctly different from what it is at work—just an item to be aware of if you are not already. For example, this author, as a sitting Chief of Police, was invited to a business breakfast meeting with a local politician. However, instead of just the two of us, the author was asked to bring a male colleague, as he did not dine alone with women. It was a business meal, and as a woman, I was treated differently from how a man would have been.

The network you build should include progressive thinkers who share similar views—notice the term like-minded was not used. Only associating with those who think as you do will inevitably limit your perspective and stifle both personal and professional growth. Diverse networks offer access to a broader range of insights, approaches, and lived experiences, all of which are crucial for informed decision-making and adaptive leadership in any field. It is through these varied connections that one uncovers creative solutions to complex problems, benefiting not only from shared knowledge but from the fresh perspectives that challenge standard approaches.

Strategically, building robust networks requires intention and openness. Attend conferences, participate in cross-departmental projects, and engage in professional associations to meet potential mentors, sponsors, and allies. Another method for building a robust network is to attend advanced leadership training, such as the FBI National Academy, Southern Police Institute, and the Law Enforcement Management Institute of Texas. These relationships can provide support, guidance, and tangible opportunities that might not be accessible otherwise. Additionally, do not underestimate the power of community involvement, volunteering, and serving on boards or committees. These external engagements not only expand your understanding of the challenges faced by different groups but also increase visibility and credibility within and beyond your immediate sphere.

It is also important to actively seek out individuals with diverse viewpoints—whether from different backgrounds, industries, or generations. Engaging with those who question or constructively critique your ideas cultivates resilience and adaptability, sharpening your leadership acumen. As you widen your circle, remember that authenticity is key; relationships built on genuine respect and mutual benefit are far more durable and impactful than those established solely for transactional gain.

Finally, recognize that these networks are not static; they require nurturing and regular investment of time and effort. Make it a habit to reach out, offer support, share resources, and celebrate others' milestones. In doing so, you contribute to a culture of reciprocity, which not only supports your own journey but also fosters the advancement of everyone connected to you. By embracing the richness and diversity of broad, strategic networks, you position yourself—and those around you—for long-term success, greater innovation, and collective resilience. Be the woman who tells another woman her crown is crooked, but don't tell everyone else.

CHAPTER 4

THE 'IT' FACTOR

*"Chiefs who possess
'It' are defined not solely by the authority of their
office, but…"*

What, precisely, is "It"? The term refers to the distinctive and rarely found combination of traits that enable a Chief of Police to lead with strength, clarity, and conscience. "It" cannot be reduced to a single characteristic or technical skill; rather, it reflects a comprehensive integration of leadership capacity, ethical grounding, and a deep commitment to public service. Chiefs who possess "It" are defined not solely by the authority of their office, but by their ability to inspire trust, advance justice, and cultivate resilience within their departments and communities.

At its essence, "It" is an enduring dedication to public service. Chiefs who embody these qualities understand that law enforcement leadership is not an exercise in power but a responsibility to serve with fairness and integrity. She recognizes that every directive issued, every strategic decision made, and every word spoken reverberates through the ranks of the department and into the broader community. The influence of a chief with "It" extends far beyond administrative oversight—it shapes the very culture of policing itself.

"It" is a term that encapsulates the essence of what makes an exceptional Chief of Police. It is difficult to define in a single word or phrase because it is not just one quality—it is the sum of many. "It" is the intangible, yet observable, presence of leadership, character, discipline, vision, and integrity wrapped into one role. "It" is what differentiates a good chief from a great one. Moreover, while the ability to lead others is central to this role, leadership alone cannot ensure success. A Chief of Police must embody a broad and deeply interconnected set of qualities that enable them to navigate the complex and often challenging landscape of modern policing.

The most successful Chiefs of Police are those who go beyond management and administration. She leads from the front, communicates with clarity, and inspires through their actions. She must be able to respond to crises, foster community trust, implement change, manage staff, and enforce discipline—often all in the same day. The foundation for all of this rests on a series of essential traits: the ability to communicate effectively, exercise administrative oversight, build interpersonal relationships, foster creativity, exhibit confidence while maintaining humility, uphold professionalism, and display unshakable resilience. But above all else, the cornerstone of a great Chief of Police is integrity.

Leadership: Leading People, Not Just Managing Them

Leadership is not just about rank or position—it is about influence, guidance, and inspiration. A Chief must understand that leadership involves **leading people**, not merely **managing them**. This distinction is vital. You manage resources like budgets, vehicles, and schedules, but you lead people—officers, staff, and members of the community. A Chief of Police must possess the capacity to inspire trust, loyalty, and dedication from those they lead. This comes from consistent behavior, ethical decision-making, and an unwavering commitment to doing the right thing.

Leadership at this level requires emotional intelligence, sound judgment, and a calm presence, especially during times of uncertainty. It also demands the courage to make difficult decisions, even when those decisions may be unpopular. Whether it is disciplining an officer for misconduct or standing firm on an unpopular reform, great Chiefs do not shy away from their responsibilities. She understands that authentic leadership sometimes means standing alone, so long as they stand on principles that are moral, legal, and ethical.

In leading people, Chiefs must create a culture of accountability and excellence. This means setting high expectations but also giving officers the support and tools needed to meet them. A leader inspires through their own example—by being punctual, prepared, responsive, and ethical at all times. Leading is also continually advocating for your personnel. Policing is difficult, and these men and women need a strong leader to advocate for them on all fronts.

Communication: The Bridge Between Vision and Action

No Chief can lead effectively without mastering the art of communication. This goes beyond simply issuing orders. Effective communication involves conveying complex ideas clearly, listening with empathy, and adapting one's message to the audience. A Chief of Police must speak confidently and clearly when addressing their department, city officials, or the public, but they must also be skilled at listening—truly listening—to the concerns, fears, and hopes of those they serve.

Good communication builds bridges—between the department and the community, between leadership and rank-and-file officers, and between law enforcement and elected officials. It requires transparency, clarity, and responsiveness. Whether she is delivering a press briefing following a critical incident, meeting with concerned residents after a controversial arrest, or conducting a performance evaluation for a new officer, the Chief's words carry weight.

Effective communication also plays a key role in de-escalation and conflict resolution. Chiefs who model calm, respectful dialogue help foster a departmental culture where communication becomes a tool for safety, respect, and progress.

Administrative Oversight: Vision with Execution

A Chief of Police wears many hats, but few are as critical as that of an administrator. At the helm of a complex public safety organization, the Chief must ensure that every element of the department is functioning efficiently and lawfully. This includes oversight of finances, resources, staffing, compliance, and internal policies. It means crafting policies that are not only legally sound but also reflective of community expectations and values.

Administrative oversight is not glamorous, but it is foundational. It is the difference between a department that functions like a finely tuned machine and one that collapses under the weight of disorganization and inefficiency. Chiefs must be familiar with budgeting processes, procurement policies, human resource management, collective bargaining agreements, and federal, State, and local statutes. She must also monitor emerging trends—such as technological advancements, advances in forensics or data analytics—and guide her departments in adopting these tools wisely.

As retired Chief Gene Ellis(ret.) aptly stated, "Inspect what you expect." Chiefs must not only set the standard but also follow through with inspections, audits, and evaluations to ensure that expectations are being met. The Chief must continually ask, "Are we achieving what we set out to do?" and if not, "Why not, and what can we do about it?"

Interpersonal Skills: Building Trust Inside and Out

Interpersonal skills are the glue that binds a leader's vision to effective action. A Chief must know how to build trust—not just command respect. Trust is earned through consistency, empathy, and transparency. Chiefs with strong interpersonal skills can resolve conflicts, foster teamwork, and build consensus even when opinions differ sharply.

Internally, a Chief must establish a strong rapport with their officers, command staff, and civilian employees. She should know their people—not just their ranks or job titles, but their strengths, their struggles, and their motivations. While knowing everyone is not possible in larger organizations, a quick handwritten note when good news reaches the chief's desk goes a long way. Recognizing and affirming good work, listening to concerns, and demonstrating fairness in discipline are all part of this relationship-building. Take care of your people. Again, take care of your people. Go to bat for them when they are right, hold them accountable when they aren't. Seek better working conditions, compensation, and equipment when it is needed. Ask yourself this question: "Do I know the name of the person who cleans our building?" It is always a good idea to put names to the faces.

Externally, Chiefs are the face of the department. She must work hand in hand with community leaders, business owners, clergy, activists, educators, and elected officials. She must be able to connect across cultural, economic, and political divides and represent the department in a manner that reflects respect, accountability, and compassion. Building social equity is a great way to weather storms when they arise. The time to meet your community is before it hits the fan, and it will hit the fan. Get out from behind the desk and get out of the office.

Interpersonal savvy also includes emotional regulation. A great Chief knows how to stay calm under pressure and model professionalism, especially when tensions run high. You may have lots to say, but engage thy brain before running thy mouth. This pause will save you in the long run, trust me.

Some years ago, my chief was out of town and left me in charge. I was performing my job and hers for about a week. In the midst of all of the regular whirlwind duties, I had to complete an extensive report to the Council. One Councilmember had numerous questions and requested additional data, but there was no time to obtain it. I informed my Chief, and she told me not to put too much effort into it, as he probably wouldn't read it anyway. My mistake when I talked to this Councilmember again was not filtering her message. I did not engage my brain before engaging my mouth. When I presented this report to Council, this particular member asked me questions for over an hour. This was an interpersonal skill failure, and one I never made again.

Creativity: Innovation in a World of Constraints

Policing is an evolving profession, and Chiefs must be at the forefront of innovation. In an age when departments are expected to do more with less—less money, fewer staff, and, at times, less public support—creativity becomes an essential leadership trait. Creativity involves finding new ways to solve old problems, whether it is reducing crime, improving officer wellness, or engaging disaffected youth.

Creative Chiefs look beyond traditional enforcement models. She considers strategies like problem-oriented policing, community-led initiatives, and restorative justice. She encourages officers to participate in brainstorming and solution development. She supports experimentation—understanding that not every new idea will work, but that stagnation is a greater risk than failure.

Creativity also means being flexible. When a traditional patrol approach fails to reduce neighborhood crime, perhaps a foot patrol combined with community meetings will have better results. When budget constraints make hiring difficult, perhaps a public-private partnership can fund necessary technology upgrades. The creative Chief is always asking: "Is there a better way?" Don't constantly bring up what was done at a previous agency, and do not fall into the trap of doing something "because it has always been done this way" if you promoted through the ranks at one agency.

Confidence and Humility: The Leadership Balancing Act

It may seem paradoxical, but confidence and humility must coexist within a Chief of Police. Confidence is necessary to lead—to step forward during chaos, to speak with conviction, and to make unpopular decisions when they are the right ones. But humility ensures that this confidence does not turn into arrogance. Humility does not make a chief weak; it exudes strength.

As Arnold H. Glasow said, "A good leader takes a little more than his share of the blame and a little less than his share of the credit." This humble posture allows the Chief to foster a healthy culture within the department, where ideas can flow from all levels and officers feel valued for their contributions.

Confidence empowers the Chief to stand before a skeptical crowd and explain departmental decisions with clarity and conviction. Humility, on the other hand, allows the Chief to acknowledge when mistakes are made and to listen—truly listen—to those impacted. A Chief who exudes both traits can lead a department that is both proud and introspective, strong yet compassionate.

Resilience: Endurance in the Face of Crisis

Law enforcement leadership is rarely predictable. Chiefs may find themselves navigating civil unrest, internal scandals, budget crises, natural disasters, officer-involved shootings, or even personal attacks on their character or decisions. In these moments, resilience becomes paramount.

A resilient Chief is one who can absorb criticism without becoming defensive, endure setbacks without losing morale, and adapt to changing conditions without compromising core values. Resilience does not mean ignoring stress—it means managing it. It means surrounding oneself with trusted advisors, knowing when to delegate, and practicing self-care to remain grounded.

It also means having friends outside of law enforcement, having hobbies, and taking your vacation time to unplug.

Resilience also includes the ability to instill hope and purpose in others. After a department experiences trauma—such as the loss of an officer in the line of duty or a deeply controversial incident—a resilient Chief becomes the rock that others look to. Through words, presence, and actions, they help the department grieve, reflect, and rebuild.

Professionalism: The Standard of Excellence

Professionalism is more than appearance—it is about conduct, ethics, and consistency. A Chief who exemplifies professionalism sets the tone for how every officer in the department will behave, particularly in moments of stress or scrutiny. She treats all individuals—regardless of rank, background, or behavior—with fairness and dignity.

Professionalism means showing up prepared, conducting oneself with decorum, and honoring commitments. It also includes continuing education—being a lifelong learner who stays abreast of trends, challenges, and evolving public expectations. A professional Chief leads not just with authority but with earned credibility. Their demeanor, decisions, and language consistently reflect their role not just as enforcers of law, but as stewards of justice.

Integrity: The Bedrock of Law Enforcement Leadership

If there is one trait that cannot be compromised—ever—it is integrity. A Chief of Police's integrity is the foundation upon which all other qualities rest. It is the central pillar that supports leadership, decision-making, communication, and public trust.

Integrity means being honest, consistent, and ethical. It means adhering to a moral compass even when no one is watching, and especially when everyone is. A Chief with integrity holds themselves and their department accountable. She does not bend to political winds, nor does she apply rules selectively.

The Chief is the final word on many matters of discipline, policy, and public representation. If her integrity is in question, then every decision she makes becomes suspect. As Abraham Lincoln wisely said, "Nearly all men can stand adversity, but if you want to test a man's character, give him power."

A Chief's power is immense—and so is the potential for misuse. That is why integrity is the non-negotiable. A department can recover from budget shortfalls or staffing shortages. It can even recover from a scandal. But a Chief who loses integrity may never regain the complete trust of the department or the community. Once questioned, integrity is never again whole.

Defining "It": The Essence of Police Leadership

A Chief of Police sets the tone, pace, and expectations for the entire department. The individual occupying this role is not simply an administrator; she serves as a strategist, mentor, problem-solver, and custodian of the public trust. Her leadership style becomes the model for officers to build their own approach to service. When a chief consistently demonstrates fairness, accountability, and empathy, those values cascade through the department and guide interactions with the public. Conversely, when leadership is absent or inconsistent, organizational culture may deteriorate, and the trust essential to effective policing is weakened.

Chapter 5

Skillsets needed

"Chiefs must be able to synthesize complex information, consider diverse perspectives, and make informed choices…"

Becoming a Chief of Police requires a comprehensive skill set that encompasses various areas of expertise, leadership qualities, and interpersonal abilities. Here are some key skills needed for success.

Law Enforcement Experience: Extensive experience in law enforcement is essential, including a thorough understanding of policing principles, procedures, and regulations. Successful Chiefs of Police have well-rounded careers, having spent time in various divisions. Well-rounded knowledge does not mean all-knowing; it simply means having an understanding of the operations of the agency as a whole instead of a limited scope. Promoting through the ranks provides supervisory experience at various levels within the agency, and increased responsibilities prepare those aspiring to be chief. In addition to the technical aspects of policing, becoming a police administrator necessitates a knowledge of administrative experience, such as budgeting, policy development, and employee discipline.

Strong leadership and management skills are crucial for effectively leading a law enforcement agency. Chiefs must be able to inspire and motivate their teams, fostering a sense of shared purpose and commitment to the agency's mission. This involves not only setting a clear vision but also communicating it in a way that resonates with officers and staff at all levels. Effective chiefs lead by example, demonstrating integrity, accountability, and resilience in the face of challenges. She must make tough decisions, often under pressure, balancing the needs of the department, the expectations of the community, and the realities of limited resources.

Strategic Planning and Decision Making: Chiefs of Police must be adept at developing and executing strategic plans that not only align with the department's mission but also respond effectively to the evolving needs of the community. This process begins with a thorough assessment of the department's current capabilities, resources, and challenges. Chiefs are responsible for setting clear, measurable goals that reflect both short-term priorities and long-term visions for public safety and organizational growth. These goals should be informed by data analysis, community feedback, and an understanding of broader societal trends that may impact law enforcement.

Effective strategic planning requires chiefs to anticipate potential risks and obstacles, ranging from budget constraints and staffing shortages to emerging crime patterns and technological changes. Chiefs must evaluate these risks carefully, weighing the possible outcomes of various courses of action. This involves consulting with command staff, engaging with community stakeholders, and reviewing best practices from other agencies.

Decision-making in this context is both an art and a science. Chiefs must be able to synthesize complex information, consider diverse perspectives, and make informed choices that advance the department's objectives while maintaining public trust. This means being proactive in identifying opportunities for innovation, such as adopting new policing strategies, implementing advanced technologies, or fostering partnerships with local organizations. It also requires the ability to respond decisively during crises, ensuring that actions taken are consistent with departmental values and legal standards.

Ultimately, strategic planning and decision-making are ongoing processes. Chiefs must regularly review progress toward established goals, adjust plans as circumstances change, and communicate updates transparently to both internal teams and the public. By leading with vision, adaptability, and integrity, Chiefs of Police can guide their departments toward greater effectiveness, resilience, and community engagement.

Communication and Interpersonal Skills: Effective communication skills are essential for Chiefs of Police to convey information clearly, build relationships with stakeholders, and inspire trust within the community. Chiefs must be adept at both public speaking and interpersonal communication. This means not only being able to articulate departmental goals, policies, and expectations in a way that is accessible and motivating, but also being a careful and empathetic listener who values input from officers, staff, and community members alike.

A Chief's communication responsibilities extend far beyond issuing directives or making public statements. She must be able to translate complex law enforcement concepts into language that resonates with diverse audiences, including city officials, the media, advocacy groups, and residents from all walks of life. This requires adaptability—knowing when to be formal and authoritative, and when to be approachable and conversational. Chiefs are often called upon to address the public during times of crisis or controversy, where their ability to communicate transparently and calmly can help maintain public confidence and de-escalate tensions.

Interpersonal skills are equally critical. Chiefs must foster positive relationships within the department, encouraging open dialogue, collaboration, and mutual respect among officers and civilian employees. By building rapport and trust, they create an environment where team members feel valued and empowered to share concerns or innovative ideas. Externally, Chiefs serve as the face of the department, engaging with community leaders, business owners, educators, and faith-based organizations to build partnerships that enhance public safety and community well-being.

Moreover, effective Chiefs recognize the importance of nonverbal communication—body language, tone of voice, and presence—which can often speak louder than words. She is skilled at reading the room and adjusting her approach based on the needs and emotions of those she is addressing. In challenging situations, such as mediating conflicts or responding to community grievances, strong interpersonal skills enable

Chiefs to demonstrate empathy, fairness, and a genuine commitment to finding solutions.

Ultimately, communication and interpersonal skills are foundational to successful leadership in law enforcement. These traits enable Chiefs to bridge gaps between the department and the community, foster a culture of transparency and accountability, and inspire confidence in their ability to lead with integrity and vision.

Crisis Management: Chiefs of Police must be prepared to handle crises and emergencies effectively, making swift and decisive decisions under pressure while maintaining calm and composure. In the dynamic and unpredictable environment of law enforcement, crises can arise at any moment—ranging from natural disasters and public safety threats to internal departmental issues or high-profile incidents that attract media attention. The ability to respond quickly and thoughtfully is essential, as the decisions made during these critical moments can have far-reaching consequences for the department, the community, and public trust.

Effective crisis management begins with thorough preparation and planning. Chiefs must ensure that their departments have clear protocols and contingency plans in place for a variety of emergency scenarios. This includes conducting regular training exercises, fostering strong communication channels among officers and staff, and building collaborative relationships with other agencies and community partners. By proactively preparing for potential crises, Chiefs can help minimize confusion and ensure a coordinated response when emergencies occur.

During a crisis, Chiefs must demonstrate exceptional leadership by remaining calm and focused, even when faced with intense scrutiny or rapidly changing circumstances. She must be able to quickly assess complex situations, gather relevant information, and consult with key stakeholders to make informed decisions. This often involves balancing competing priorities, such as protecting public safety, supporting officers, and maintaining transparency with the community and media.

Decisive action is crucial, but so is adaptability. Chiefs must be willing to adjust their strategies as new information emerges and conditions evolve. She should communicate clearly and consistently with both internal teams and external audiences, providing updates, addressing concerns, and explaining the rationale behind their decisions. Maintaining composure and demonstrating empathy during difficult times helps to reassure the public and foster trust in law enforcement leadership.

After the immediate crisis has passed, Chiefs must lead efforts to review and evaluate the department's response. This includes identifying lessons learned, implementing improvements, and supporting officers and community members affected by the event. By embracing a culture of continuous improvement and accountability, Chiefs can strengthen their department's resilience and readiness for future challenges.

Ultimately, crisis management and decision-making are defining aspects of police leadership. Chiefs who excel in these areas not only protect their communities during emergencies but also set a standard for professionalism, integrity, and effective governance within their agencies.

Ethical Leadership and Integrity: Upholding high ethical standards is paramount for Chiefs of Police, who serve as role models for their departments and the community. The Chief of Police is not only responsible for enforcing the law but also for setting the moral tone and ethical expectations for the entire organization. Integrity, honesty, and transparency are essential qualities for earning and maintaining public trust, and these values must be demonstrated consistently in both words and actions.

A Chief's ethical leadership is reflected in every decision made, from the way policies are developed and enforced to how officers are held accountable for their conduct. Chiefs must ensure that their own behavior is above reproach, as their actions are closely scrutinized by officers, city officials, and the public alike. This means being transparent about departmental operations, openly communicating about challenges and mistakes, and taking responsibility for both successes and failures.

Furthermore, ethical leadership involves fostering a culture in which officers feel empowered to speak up about wrongdoing without fear of retaliation. Chiefs must establish clear channels for reporting misconduct and ensure that all complaints are investigated thoroughly and impartially. By fostering an environment of accountability and fairness, Chiefs help build a department where ethical behavior is the norm rather than the exception.

In addition, Chiefs must navigate complex ethical dilemmas, balancing the needs of the community, the rights of individuals, and the demands of the law. This requires sound judgment, empathy, and a steadfast commitment to doing what is right, even when it is difficult or unpopular. Chiefs who prioritize ethical leadership inspire confidence among their officers and the public, reinforcing the legitimacy of the police department and strengthening the social contract between law enforcement and the community.

Ultimately, the legacy of a Chief of Police is defined not just by crime statistics or operational achievements, but by the integrity with which she leads. By upholding the highest ethical standards, Chiefs set a powerful example for others to follow and ensure that their departments are trusted, respected, and effective in serving the public good.

Community Engagement and Relationship Building: Chiefs of Police must actively engage with the community, listening to concerns, building partnerships, and fostering positive relationships to promote public safety and trust. This engagement goes far beyond attending public meetings or issuing statements; it requires a genuine commitment to understanding the unique needs, perspectives, and challenges faced by diverse groups within the community. Chiefs should prioritize regular, open communication with residents, business owners, faith leaders, educators, and advocacy organizations, ensuring that all voices are heard and valued.

Building strong partnerships involves collaborating with local organizations, government agencies, and community groups to address public safety issues collectively. Chiefs can initiate and participate in outreach programs, educational workshops, and community forums that encourage dialogue and transparency. By being visible and approachable, Chiefs demonstrate their dedication to serving not just as law enforcers, but as trusted members of the community.

Fostering positive relationships also means responding proactively to concerns and feedback, whether related to crime prevention, officer conduct, or broader social issues. Chiefs should work to create opportunities for meaningful interaction, such as neighborhood walks, youth engagement initiatives, and cultural events that celebrate the diversity of the community. These efforts help to break down barriers, dispel misconceptions, and build mutual respect between law enforcement and the public.

Ultimately, effective community engagement and relationship building are foundational to promoting public safety and trust. When Chiefs invest in these relationships, they not only enhance the legitimacy of their departments but also empower communities to play an active role in shaping the future of policing. This collaborative approach leads to stronger partnerships, improved problem-solving, and a safer, more unified community.

Conflict Resolution and Problem-Solving: Chiefs of Police must possess strong conflict resolution skills to address internal disputes, community tensions, and other challenges effectively. The ability to resolve conflicts is not only essential for maintaining harmony within the department but also for fostering trust and cooperation with the broader community. Chiefs are often called upon to mediate disagreements between officers, handle grievances from staff, and respond to concerns raised by citizens or community groups. This requires a calm, impartial approach, as well as the capacity to listen actively and empathize with all parties involved.

In addition to resolving interpersonal disputes, Chiefs must be adept at managing larger-scale conflicts that may arise from controversial incidents, policy changes, or shifts in community expectations. She needs to facilitate open dialogue, encourage transparency, and ensure that all voices are heard during the resolution process. By promoting a culture of respect and accountability, Chiefs can help prevent minor disagreements from escalating into major issues that could undermine departmental morale or public confidence.

Problem-solving is equally critical in the role of Chief of Police. Chiefs must be skilled at identifying the root causes of complex issues, whether they involve operational inefficiencies, resource constraints, or emerging crime trends. This involves gathering and analyzing relevant data, consulting with subject matter experts, and considering input from both internal and external stakeholders. Chiefs should approach problems with creativity and adaptability, exploring innovative solutions and best practices from other agencies when appropriate.

Implementing effective solutions requires strategic planning and clear communication. Chiefs must be able to articulate the rationale behind their decisions, set measurable goals, and monitor progress to ensure that interventions are successful. She should also be prepared to adjust strategies as circumstances evolve, demonstrating flexibility and resilience in the face of new challenges. Strong conflict resolution and problem-solving skills enable Chiefs of Police to lead their departments with confidence, maintain positive relationships within the organization and the community, and ensure that complex issues are addressed in a timely and constructive manner.

Adaptability and Innovation: Law enforcement is a dynamic and ever-evolving field, requiring Chiefs of Police to be highly adaptable to a wide range of changing circumstances, emerging trends, and new technologies. The landscape of public safety is continually shaped by societal shifts, legislative updates, technological advancements, and evolving community expectations.

Chiefs must be prepared to respond proactively to these changes, adjusting departmental strategies and policies to remain effective and relevant in serving their communities.

Being adaptive means being open to new ideas and approaches, even when they challenge long-standing traditions or established practices within the department. Chiefs who embrace adaptability are willing to reassess current procedures, learn from both successes and setbacks, and implement changes that enhance operational efficiency and community relations. This flexibility is especially crucial when navigating unexpected events, such as public health crises, shifts in crime patterns, or changes in local government priorities. An important note: evaluate before making changes, if possible.

Innovation goes hand in hand with adaptability. Forward-thinking Chiefs actively seek out and implement new technologies, such as advanced data analytics, body-worn cameras, and modern communication tools, to improve policing practices and outcomes. She encourages a culture of creativity within their teams, empowering officers and staff to propose innovative solutions to persistent challenges. By fostering an environment where innovation is valued and learning from failure is accepted, Chiefs can drive continuous improvement and keep their departments at the forefront of best practices.

Furthermore, Chiefs who prioritize adaptability and innovation are better equipped to address complex issues like community trust, officer wellness, and resource constraints. They are more likely to build partnerships with other agencies, community organizations, and technology providers, leveraging collective expertise to solve problems collaboratively. This openness to collaboration and new perspectives not only strengthens the department but also enhances its ability to serve and protect the public effectively. Adaptability and innovation are not just desirable traits—they are essential for Chiefs of Police who aim to lead resilient, responsive, and forward-looking law enforcement agencies in today's rapidly changing world.

Political Acumen and Advocacy: This is often overlooked. Chiefs of Police often work closely with elected officials, government agencies, and community leaders. Political acumen and advocacy skills are valuable for navigating political dynamics, securing resources, and advocating for policies that support public safety. Building social equity begins on day 1 of the job. You are going to need it at some point.

Chapter 6

Preparing for the process

"...still want to be a Chief of Police, you need to prepare for the struggles and hurdles."

If you are still reading and, after all of the skills needed, barriers, and derailers, you still want to be a Chief of Police, you need to prepare for the struggles and hurdles of the application and interview processes. Once you have identified an opportunity you want to explore, do some research. There is a lot of information available on the internet, especially on the entity's website and its social media pages. Meeting agendas and minutes provide a great deal of information, as do meeting recordings. Do not limit the search to City Council; also consider other boards and commissions, such as Planning and Zoning, for future growth in the area. Review the budgets and familiarize yourself with the departmental budget. What organizations are in the city (Lions, Rotary, etc.)? The Chamber of Commerce is also a good source of information. If possible, drive around the area and get a feel for the community. Get out of the car, eat a meal in the city, and visit a shop or two to learn more. If, after conducting the research, you are satisfied with what you have learned, begin the application process.

Most processes begin with the submission of a cover letter and resume. Sometimes an application is also required. Those making the first cut are often asked to complete a narrative questionnaire. Some of the types of questions asked are:

1. Please outline the reason(s) you left your last three positions.

2. Are there gaps of over two weeks in your employment history? If so, please explain in detail.

3. What does "community policing" mean to you, and how do you ensure that police employees incorporate and apply this philosophy? Please provide specific examples of your work.

4. How do you personally define leadership? Please provide an example of a time when you have led a group. What were the circumstances, what specific actions did you take, and what was the eventual outcome?

5. Describe your work in creating and maintaining strong community relationships. Please provide specific examples.

6. Describe the vision, mission, and values of your current organization. Describe how you bring these concepts to life in your current role. Please provide specific examples.

7. What are the three most important questions you would have for the City Manager or person responsible for hiring?

8. Please explain in your words what you believe the role of Chief of Police with the _____ Police Department should be.

9. Describe your leadership philosophy and how it develops the internal culture to meet the expectations of the community.

10. As Chief, citizens will come to you to complain about the actions or behavior of your officers. In discussing such complaints with these individuals, what should your priority be?

11. Describe the relationship that should exist between officials of the police department and officials of other divisions of the entity (city government, college or university, etc.) as it relates to serving the public and to public policy.

12. Describe the most effective supervisor you have ever worked for, and what there was about him/her that was so special (No names, please).

13. Describe the most prominent internal challenges the next Chief will face. What problems can be anticipated, and how can they be dealt with?

14. What would your peers and subordinates say are your strengths?

15. What can you do as a Chief to improve staff retention?

16. Please list your next three top priorities during your first 90 days if you are selected as Chief.

This list is not exhaustive but provides specific examples of what a candidate can be expected to respond to. If you choose not to answer these questions in writing now, think about what your answers would be for the future.

The cover letter should include a brief overview of your career and why you are the most qualified for the position. The cover letter should state the purpose of the letter, tenure in the profession, and educational highlights. It should also include specific accomplishments and career focal points. Additionally, discuss any involvement in professional organizations. An example of a cover letter is included in the text for reference.

The resume can take many forms. The most common types are chronological, functional, and combination. The chronological resume lists the most recent position and experience first and continues in reverse order. A functional resume focuses on skills rather than work experience. The combination resume combines aspects of the chronological and functional resumes. An example of a resume is included in the text for reference.

The documents submitted in consideration for employment must be error-free. The quality of the documents submitted is equally important as the content. Poorly written documents or documents with errors do not lend themselves to a credible candidate. There is no shame in asking someone to proofread your documents.

Chapter 7

The Interview

"Answers that are too succinct will not let your 'it' factor shine through…

The interview process can elevate blood pressure and cause some, okay, a lot of anxiety. As a female, you know you are the minority and that the competition for the position is statistically going to be mostly males. The interview can be as simple as a one-on-one with the City Manager or other hiring entity, or it could be a day-long process with interviews with multiple groups. It is also possible that the interview process will cover multiple days. Often, other department heads are part of an interview panel for candidate selection. Questions from panel members can be generic or specific. Examples of the types of questions commonly asked are:

1. Summarize your professional background
2. Tell us about yourself
3. What interested you in this position?
4. How do you keep your supervisor informed?
5. What is your approach to dealing with the recruiting crisis in policing?
6. What size budget do you currently manage?
7. Describe your leadership style.
8. What is your most important professional accomplishment?

9. What research have you done on the employing entity (city, college, university, etc.) and/or the agency?

10. Have you reviewed the budget?

11. What are your strengths?

12. What are your weaknesses?

Another less formal part of the interview process may also be included. This is a meet-and-greet with specific community members and members of the governing body or an open-to-the-public event. These events are less structured, and the questions are wide-ranging. Be cautious, however. While less formal and non-structured, these interviews are an important part of the process. The manager will listen to the opinions of those invited on how you interact with those in attendance.

Lastly, whether the interview is a one-on-one interview with the manager or a panel interview, answer the questions asked, but treat the process like a conversation by adding relevant examples. Avoid the mistake of answering the questions as if you are sitting for a deposition. The interview should be an exchange of information. Answers that are too succinct will not let your "it" factor shine through, which would be a disservice to yourself. Let the information flow freely, providing complete answers with examples when possible. This is the perfect time to be confident and highlight your achievements while still exhibiting the humility of a servant leader.

Chapter 8

You Have an Offer; Now What?

"This moment is not just ceremonial, it is strategic."

After weeks or even months of preparation, anticipation, and interviews, the phone call finally arrives: *you are the choice to lead the police department.* Few moments in a career carry such weight. The offer to serve as Chief of Police represents both the culmination of years of service and the beginning of an entirely new challenge. Along with the congratulations will come the details of a compensation package—salary, benefits, and sometimes additional incentives. While the offer may be generous, it may not initially address all of your needs or expectations.

This moment is not just ceremonial; it is strategic. It is also the time when you will have the most negotiating power. Before signing a contract or making a verbal commitment, it is essential to evaluate the offer with care. What you accept now will shape your ability to succeed later. This is the window in which you must ask for what you need—not only for yourself but for the effectiveness of your leadership and the health of the organization you are about to serve.

Timing – This is one of the most common mistakes new chiefs make. It is delaying difficult conversations about compensation and benefits. It can be tempting to accept the offer immediately out of excitement, gratitude, or concern about appearing demanding. However, waiting six months or a year to request more vacation time, additional retirement contributions, or professional development support is rarely effective. Once the agreement is finalized, your leverage decreases significantly.

The negotiation phase is the time to speak openly and clearly about your expectations. Doing so does not signal greed or arrogance; it reflects professionalism and foresight. The city or governing body has identified you as their top choice for a reason. They want you in the role, and they want you to succeed. In most cases, the hiring authority is prepared for some level of negotiation. A thoughtful, respectful discussion at this stage lays the foundation for transparency and mutual respect.

Understanding the Context

Be sure to understand the context of the discussions. In some entities, the selection process involves a "top two" scenario, where both finalists are under consideration until the agreement is finalized. In such cases, it can feel risky to negotiate firmly, knowing another candidate is still in the background. Even here, remember that you were named the number one choice for specific reasons. The governing body or city manager has concluded that your skills, leadership, and vision make you the best fit for the organization. Chiefs are not interchangeable; the selection is deliberate.

The appointment of a police chief is one of the most consequential hires an entity can make. Chiefs are among the most visible leaders in local government. They are expected to serve as the face of the department, the manager of its operations, the steward of public trust, and the voice of accountability during crises. Because of this, entities are often willing to provide additional incentives to secure the right candidate.

Areas for Negotiation

When evaluating an offer, consider more than base salary. Chiefs of Police carry unique responsibilities, and their contracts should reflect that. Areas to review and, if necessary, negotiate include:

- **Salary and Adjustments:** Ensure the starting salary is competitive with chiefs in comparable jurisdictions. Ask whether performance-based

increases or cost-of-living adjustments are included.
- **Retirement Contributions:** Request clarification about pension eligibility, buyback options, or enhanced contributions, especially if you are nearing the end of your career.
- **Vacation and Leave:** Confirm how much vacation time is provided and whether it aligns with the demands of the role. Chiefs need recovery time to remain effective.
- **Professional Development:** Negotiate for support to attend executive training programs, national policing conferences, or leadership institutes.
- **Relocation Assistance:** If moving to a new jurisdiction, relocation expenses, temporary housing, or even spousal employment support may be available.
- **Contract Length and Renewal Terms:** Multi-year agreements provide stability, especially in politically dynamic environments.
- **Severance Provisions:** Because chiefs serve at the pleasure of elected officials, severance packages protect both you and your family in the event of abrupt leadership transitions.

Negotiation as a Leadership Skill

For many leaders, particularly women, asking for what they want can feel uncomfortable. Cultural expectations, previous experiences, or concerns about being perceived as "difficult" often create hesitation. Yet negotiation is not a selfish act; it is a leadership skill. If you cannot advocate for yourself at the outset, how will you advocate for the needs of your department once in the role?

Approach negotiation with preparation and professionalism—research comparable contracts in similar municipalities. Identify the provisions that are most important to you. Prioritize them, and be ready to explain why they matter not only to your well-being but also to your ability to serve effectively.

For example, framing vacation time as essential for sustaining long-term resilience demonstrates foresight, not indulgence. Positioning professional development funding as a means of bringing best practices back to the department underscores a commitment to excellence.

Sample Negotiation Phrasing

The way you articulate requests matters. Here are examples of how a chief can negotiate with confidence and diplomacy:

- **On Salary**
  "I appreciate the offer and the confidence you

have placed in me. I have reviewed comparable chief positions in cities of similar size, and I would like to discuss a salary adjustment to ensure this role is aligned with the market."

- **On Retirement**
"Given where I am in my career, retirement contributions are a significant factor in my decision. I want to explore whether the city could increase contributions or provide credit for prior service."

- **On Vacation/Leave**
"The responsibilities of this role are demanding, and ensuring I have the opportunity to recharge is essential for sustained effectiveness. I want to request an additional week of vacation time annually."

- **On Professional Development**
"I believe it is important to stay connected to best practices and national standards. Would the entity be open to providing funding for my attendance at one national conference and one executive leadership program each year?"

- **On Relocation Assistance**
"Relocating is a significant transition for my family. I would like to request assistance with moving expenses and temporary housing to ensure a smooth start."

- **On Contract Length/Severance**
"Given the importance of continuity in this position, I would like to discuss a three-year contract with a defined severance clause to ensure stability for both myself and the entity."

Notice that each statement is framed respectfully, with reasoning tied to effectiveness, fairness, or alignment with best practices. This tone demonstrates professionalism and reduces the likelihood of pushback.

The Tone of Negotiation

The manner in which you negotiate is as important as the content of your requests. Be assertive, but not adversarial. Demonstrate that your goal is to reach an agreement that benefits both you and the organization. Express enthusiasm for the role while also clearly articulating your needs. This approach signals confidence, professionalism, and a collaborative spirit. Avoid ultimatums or unreasonable demands, which can damage trust before your tenure even begins—instead, frame negotiation as a mutual investment. You are prepared to commit your skills, vision, and energy to the entity; in return, you ask for a contract that equips you to do so effectively.

Preparing for the Transition

Once terms are agreed upon and the contract (if applicable) is signed, the nature of the relationship shifts from negotiation to partnership. The manager or governing body becomes your employer, and your focus must turn to building trust and credibility within the organization and the community. A well-negotiated contract provides the foundation for this transition, allowing you to begin your tenure with clarity and confidence.

Final Thoughts

The offer to become a Chief of Police is one of the most significant milestones in a law enforcement career. Accepting that offer without careful negotiation can set limits on your success before you even begin. This is the moment when you have the most significant leverage; use it wisely, but never abuse it. Remember: you were chosen for a reason. You were identified as the leader best suited to guide the department and represent the community. The entity wants you in this role and will often be willing to meet reasonable requests to ensure your success.

For many women, the negotiation table may feel like unfamiliar or even uncomfortable territory. Nevertheless, it is here that you set the tone for your leadership. By asking for what you need with confidence, professionalism, and respect, you demonstrate the very qualities that made you the top choice. Negotiation is not about self-interest—it is about ensuring that you are positioned to serve with strength, clarity, and integrity. Accept the offer with pride, but only after securing the tools and terms you need to lead effectively. In doing so, you do not simply take the office; you elevate it.

Quick Reference Checklist:

Top 5 Things to Negotiate Before Accepting the Role of Chief of Police

1. **Salary and Adjustments** – Confirm competitive pay with benchmarks from similar-sized cities, and ask about cost-of-living or performance-based increases.
2. **Retirement Contributions** – Explore enhanced pension options, service credit, or higher entity contributions.
3. **Leave and Work-Life Balance** – Ensure adequate vacation, sick leave, and personal time that reflect the intensity of the role.
4. **Professional Development and Support** – Request funding for conferences, executive leadership training, and memberships in professional organizations.
5. **Contract Stability** (if applicable) – Negotiate contract length, renewal terms, and severance provisions to provide security in a politically sensitive role.

Chapter 9
You Can't Win Them All: When It All Goes South

"Understanding how to navigate those inevitable low points is as critical to long-term success as the skills that help you achieve high points."

Leadership, particularly in policing, is never a straight path of victories and applause. No matter how capable or well-prepared a chief may be, there will be moments when decisions are questioned, initiatives fail, or circumstances simply do not turn out as expected. This is not a reflection of incompetence—it is the reality of leadership in complex, high-stakes environments. Chiefs must accept an uncomfortable truth early in their tenure: *you can't win them all.*

Understanding how to navigate those inevitable low points is as critical to long-term success as the skills that help you achieve high points. Chiefs who endure and leave a meaningful legacy are not those who never face setbacks, but those who respond to setbacks with integrity, perspective, and resilience.

The Nature of the Role

The position of Chief of Police is unlike any other. Chiefs stand at the intersection of politics, law, community expectations, and organizational dynamics. She must answer to elected officials, her direct supervisor, officers, and the public simultaneously. Each of these stakeholders carries different priorities, and at times those priorities will conflict. Even the most thoughtful decision will not satisfy every group. For example, implementing stricter accountability measures may strengthen public trust but create internal resistance among officers. Conversely, prioritizing officer morale through more protective policies may generate community frustration. Chiefs must walk this tightrope knowing that complete consensus is unattainable.

When Things Go Wrong

At some point in every Chief's career, events will occur that test their resolve and leadership. These moments may include:

- **High-profile incidents:** Use-of-force cases, officer misconduct, or controversial arrests that spark public outcry.
- **Political pressure:** Conflicts with elected officials, managers, or oversight boards over policy direction or budget priorities.
- **Operational failures:** Missteps in planning, poor implementation of new programs, or breakdowns in communication.
- **Personal setbacks:** Misjudgments, communication errors, or strained relationships with key partners.

What distinguishes effective chiefs is not whether these events occur—they will—but how they respond when the tide turns.

The First Rule: Stay Grounded

When a situation begins to spiral, the instinct may be to react quickly, defend yourself aggressively, or deflect blame. These impulses are natural, but they will rarely serve you well. Chiefs who weather storms effectively remain grounded. They pause, assess the situation objectively, and resist the temptation to allow emotions to dictate their response. Remain calm under scrutiny, even when it seems unjustified. Listen, don't just listen to respond. By modeling composure, chiefs signal to both their officers and the community that the department will not be destabilized by the situation.

Accountability and Transparency

When things go south, accountability becomes non-negotiable. Minimizing or obscuring problems erodes public trust and creates long-term credibility issues. Transparency—even when uncomfortable—is the foundation for establishing, maintaining, or restoring trust. Accountability does not mean taking personal blame for every failure, but it does require owning the decisions within the Chief's authority. If an officer engages in misconduct, the Chief cannot predict or prevent every individual action. However, the Chief *can* be accountable for ensuring that policies, training, and disciplinary systems are fair and effective.

Leaders who openly acknowledge mistakes, explain corrective actions, and demonstrate a commitment to improvement often emerge stronger, even after setbacks. Let me say that again. Openly acknowledge mistakes; it's okay to say that you are sorry.

The Political Dimension

Politics plays a central role in the challenges chiefs face. A decision that aligns with best practices in law enforcement may still conflict with the priorities of a mayor, council, or manager. Chiefs must be prepared for the reality that their job security is tied not only to professional performance but also to political dynamics beyond their control. A chief, known to this author, was advised before a Council meeting that the city wanted to go in a different direction. No prior notice was given, and this chief was without a job, just like that.

When conflict arises, chiefs should maintain professionalism and focus on facts rather than personalities. Burning political bridges rarely ends well. Even if political circumstances shorten tenure, how a chief departs often matters more than the length of service. Leaving with dignity preserves your reputation and opens doors to future opportunities.

Resilience in Leadership

Setbacks test not only a chief's professional skills but also their personal resilience. Long hours, public scrutiny, and constant pressure can take a toll. Chiefs who endure adversity cultivate habits that sustain them through low points. It is imperative to have a strong support system. Faith, family, trusted mentors, and colleagues provide perspective and encouragement. It is also essential to have a good self-care routine. See your physician regularly, get plenty of rest, and avoid alcohol in excess. Utilize reflective practices to learn from mistakes and adapt your leadership approaches.

Resilience does not mean pretending challenges do not hurt. It means facing them honestly, recovering, and continuing forward with renewed determination. Challenges can cause even the best chiefs to doubt their position.

Lessons from Failure

Setbacks, while difficult, are powerful teachers. Chiefs who approach challenges as learning opportunities often emerge wiser and more effective. Some lessons commonly drawn from difficult moments include:

- **The importance of preparation:** Crises reveal weaknesses in policies, training, or communication systems.
- **The value of relationships:** Strong relationships with community leaders, elected officials, and the media can soften the impact of adverse events.
- **The need for humility:** Leaders are reminded that they cannot control every outcome and must remain adaptable.
- **The enduring value of integrity:** When all else fails, integrity remains the anchor of a chief's reputation.

You Won't Please Everyone

A core truth of leadership is that not everyone will approve of your decisions. Chiefs must resist the trap of seeking universal approval, which often leads to inconsistency or indecision. Instead, focus on making decisions grounded in principles, fairness, and the best available information. Critics will always exist. What matters is that, over time, the broader community recognizes the consistency and integrity of your leadership. Chiefs who accept that they cannot win every battle free themselves to focus on what truly matters: justice, safety, and trust.

Departures and Endings

For some chiefs, when things go south, it may lead to resignation or termination. While difficult, such endings are not career-defining unless mishandled or criminal. Many chiefs go on to successful second chapters in leadership, consulting, academia, or other public service roles. What endures is not the length of tenure but the manner of departure. Chiefs who leave with integrity—acknowledging challenges without bitterness and expressing gratitude for the opportunity—preserve their reputation and often find that future opportunities emerge precisely because of the dignity with which they handled adversity.

Practical Guidance for Chiefs

When facing setbacks, chiefs should keep the following strategies in mind:

1. **Respond, Don't React:** Take time to gather facts and perspective before making public statements.
2. **Own What You Can Control:** Accept responsibility for areas under your authority and commit to corrective action.
3. **Maintain Professionalism:** Even under criticism, avoid defensive or retaliatory behavior.
4. **Communicate Transparently:** Share information openly with both the public and the department.
5. **Lean on Relationships:** Draw upon trusted colleagues for support and advice.
6. **Prioritize Well-being:** Care for your own health and resilience to sustain effective leadership.
7. **Focus on the Long Game:** Remember that reputations are built over years, not days. One setback does not erase a career.

Final Thoughts

The phrase *"you can't win them all"* is not a concession to mediocrity—it is a recognition of the complexity of politics at the executive level. No chief can please all stakeholders, control all events, or avoid all setbacks. What defines greatness is not the absence of difficulty but the presence of integrity, resilience, and vision in the midst of it.

When things go south—as they inevitably will—the question is not whether the Chief will stumble, but whether they will rise. Chiefs who navigate adversity with humility and strength demonstrate to their officers and their communities that leadership is not about perfection, but about perseverance. They leave a legacy not of unbroken victories, but of character revealed under pressure. In the end, what matters most is not that you win every battle, but that you fight each one with fairness, clarity, and courage. Elenor Roosevelt said it best, "Do what you feel in your heart to be right, for you'll be criticized anyway. You'll be damned if you do, and damned if you don't." That is the essence of leadership, even when it all goes south.

CHAPTER 10

IS THIS THE HILL?

"...the ultimate make it or break it moment..."

The term "hill" refers to that critical point where you decide to stand your ground on a specific issue or principle—one you are willing to defend at all costs. It represents the ultimate make-or-break moment, when you are confronted with a decisive choice or challenge that could shape the outcome, define your stance, or even affect your career. This is the moment when neutrality is no longer an option, and a conscious decision is made to take a stand and refuse to back down.

Given the weight these moments carry, hills must be chosen carefully. Not every conflict deserves full engagement, and not every battle is worth the risk. The goal is to win the war, not just the immediate battle, which means exercising judgment, restraint, and strategic thinking. Emotional reactions can be powerful, especially when a situation feels personal or unjust, but leadership demands the ability to pause and assess the broader consequences.

Before choosing to take a stand, ask yourself whether the issue crosses a clear moral line. Is it immoral, unethical, or illegal? If the answer is yes, this may indeed be your hill. If not, take a long, hard look at the situation. Ask whether it will still matter in six months or a year, or whether it will fade with time and perspective. Some situations will naturally get under your skin—and sometimes rightfully so—but true wisdom lies in knowing which moments demand everything you have, and which ones are best met with patience and perspective.

CHAPTER 11

WORDS FROM THE WISE

"Don't focus on being the best female officer, just be the best officer you can be…

"Own the room without performing" – Chief Holly Green

"Never forget where you come from or the women that came before you that paved the way" – Chief Stella Bergeron Green

"Anyone seeking to advance in a policing organization needs to demonstrate operational credibility and a record of strong field performance. They should show a track record of progressive responsibility during their tenure". – Chief Todd Hunter

"Stay the course and focus on your goals while being flexible to adjusting your timelines to take advantage of opportunities that may present themselves." – Chief Gene Ellis (ret.)

"Exploit your credentials but mostly exploit your passion for the profession." – Chief John Chancellor

"Traditionally, law enforcement has been a male-dominated career field; however, in a modern, more educated society, we are progressing and seeing the benefits of women in executive leadership roles, as we fully come to understand the nature of servant leadership and emotional intelligence." – Chief Larry Berg

"Don't focus on being the best female officer, just be the best officer you can be, lean into your strengths and be aware and constantly work on improving your short falls." – Chief Jennifer Rounds

"Stay focused on your people and department; don't look for problems that are not there. Gender does not matter, leadership does. Pray for clarity, wisdom, knowledge, and discernment." – Chief Chad Taylor

"Lead with the full strength of who you are. Do not shrink to fit anyone's expectations, and do not apologize for the power of your preparation. This profession needs leaders who are transparent, respectful, engaged, emotionally intelligent, and accountable – specifically women." – Chief Sheryl Victorian

"Disregard your gender. Don't let your gender hold you back from whatever you are trying achieve. You want to be SWAT? Sign up for SWAT. You want to be a traffic officer? Sign up to be a traffic officer. Regardless of gender, we all face shortcomings or flaws we must overcome. Gender is irrelevant. Don't use it as a crutch to promote or as an excuse to avoid promoting. Follow your calling". – Chief Sonja Clay

CHAPTER 12

SUMMARY

Throughout this guide, numerous skill sets, such as leadership, integrity, and resilience, have been mentioned more than once. The reason the traits are repeated is that they are essential for success. You cannot successfully navigate the Chief of Police position without them. This guide gives you a brief look into preparing for and becoming a great Chief of Police. It will not be easy, nor should it be. If it were easy, everyone could do it, but they can't.

As a Chief, you will be responsible for all of the men and women under your command, and that is a heavy lift, but being Chief, **THE** *Ma'am In Command* is one of the most significant rewards of your career. God Bless, be safe, and best wishes on your career journey.

CHAPTER 13

EXAMPLES

Jane Smith

Jane.smith@mail.com
555-555-5555

Executive Profile

Dedicated, proactive, highly organized Chief Executive with 30 years of experience, including more than 7 years as a police chief. Proven leader with a reputation for honesty, integrity, and loyalty. Effective law enforcement professional with a proven ability to lead, train, mentor, and manage a diverse and service-oriented workforce using a Servant-Leader mindset. Innovative thinker with a background in new programs, curriculum development, and research. Excellent written and verbal communication, documentation, and personnel administration skills. A recognized and decorated leader who can create and foster an efficient and productive work environment with exceptional interpersonal and team communication levels through coaching, mentoring, and professional development of subordinates.

Career Achievements

- **Agency accreditation through the Texas Police Chiefs Association Foundation Best Practices**
- **Designed, planned, and managed the construction of a public safety facility**
- **Supervise and monitor activities of staff, including front-line and command-level personnel, providing direction and control necessary for smooth and consistent workflow and continued readiness to ensure the safety and protection of the community.**
- **Departmental policy development and implementation**
- **Development of policy and program management as Chair of UNTD's Caruth Police Institute Board**
- **Development and implementation of the state-wide mentoring program for women in law enforcement**
- **Subject-matter expert for the International Association of Chiefs of Police (IACP)**

- Curriculum development and implementation for the award-winning CSI: Camp
- Curriculum development and implementation for the Corinth and Park Place Police Department Citizens Police Academy

Professional Background

Chief of Police April 2023 to Present
Learners College Department of Public SafetyLearner, Texas

Currently serving as the Chief Executive of the Police Department, ensuring the safety and security of students, faculty, and staff. Responsible for modernizing the agency and bringing the agency into compliance with reporting requirements.

- Emergency Management
- Policy development
- Reporting compliance
- Enrolled agency for LEOSE funds
- Enrolled agency for Federal Bullet Proof Vest Partnership (BVP)
- Ensure personnel files are secured and maintained according to TCOLE rules
- Updated departmental vehicle fleet
- Updated departmental body cams, TASER devices and handheld radios

Chief of Police 2017 to 2023
City of Park Place – Police Department   Park Place, Texas

Served the citizens of Park Place as the Chief of Police. Worked as part of the City of Park Place's Executive Team, to ensure Park Place's citizens received quality customer service. Responsibilities included mentoring subordinates to develop their leadership and management skills for growth and career advancement.

- Received Texas Police Chiefs Association Foundation "Best Practices Accreditation."
- Develop policies and procedures for the Park Place Police Department

- Ensure appropriate accounting methods and controls for special use funds such as State Forfeiture, Federal Forfeiture, and State Training (LEOSE) funds
- Implemented Citizen Police Academy (CPA)
- Implemented Clergy and Police Alliance (CAPA)
- Implemented the "Take Me Home" Program
- Implemented Active Bystandership for Law Enforcement (ABLE) within the agency
- Implemented a standardized uniform policy to include issued police gear and handguns
- Established a standardized hiring process
- Established a competitive promotional process
- Entered into Interlocal Agreements for Mutual Aid and Pursuits (Greater Dallas-Fort Worth Regional Law Enforcement Mutual Aid Task Force Agreement)
- Ensured compliance with State standards and best practices in property and evidence management by hiring the subject matter expert to conduct a complete inventory, inspection, and audit
- Designed the police portion of the new Public Safety Facility
- Implemented new processes and procedures for Internal Affairs investigations
- Implemented measures to track Training, Criminal Investigation (CID) statistics, and Open Records
- Manage city-wide Enterprise lease vehicle project

Manager, Risk and Emergency Management   2016-2017
Turquoise County Schools   *Turquoise, Texas*
Served as a Risk Management team member, working to reduce the number of crashes and injuries from crashes within the District.
- Streamlined and improved school bus accident response and reporting
- Develop and implement reports to enhance the consistency in permanent accident records
- Improve tracking of discipline associated with preventable school bus accidents
- Improve tracking of discipline related to preventable school bus accidents

Lieutenant 2006 to 2016
Support Services Cornfield, *Texas*
Office of the Chief of Police
Field Operations
City of Cornfield - Police Department 1995 to 2016
Served as a member of the Executive Staff, prioritizing work schedules and delegating assignments to the appropriate personnel. A reputation as a servant leader who is fair, honest, and believes in mentoring others. Worked effectively to resolve conflicts at appropriate times. Managed budget to ensure compliance and good stewardship of public funds.
- Developed and implemented an Access database for criminal case management.
- Policy review and implementation
- 2006 Committee member, Texas Commission on Law Enforcement Officer Standards and Education (Curriculum development for new Officers)
- Community program development to include Citizens Police Academy, award-winning CSI: Camp, National Night Out
- Major case investigations
- Property and Evidence - Audits and Compliance
- Assisted in Department receiving Best Practice Recognition
- Commanded Critical Incidents
- Mentored subordinates
- Served as Field Training Administrator and monitored the progress of newly hired officers.
- Compiled data and information for the renewal of City Ordinances.
- Worked with the City Attorney on Internal Affairs Investigations, City Council presentations, and other items as required.

Education and Training

Ph.D. Candidate, Criminal Justice Leadership (33 hours completed) 2023
Bell University *Bell, Virginia*
Master of Public Administration 2007
The University of Texas at Blank *Blank, Texas*
Bachelor of Applied Arts and Sciences 2003
Western State University *Western, Texas*

Graduate, Leadership Command College (Class #174) 2025
Bill Blackwood Law Enforcement Management Institute (LEMIT) Huntsville, Texas
Graduate, School of Police Supervision 2015
Institute for Law Enforcement Administration (ILEA) Plano, Texas

Professional Affiliations and Licenses
- International Association of Chiefs of Police
- Texas Police Chiefs Association
  Board of Officers
  Ethics Committee Member
- Texas Police Chief's Association Foundation
  Board member
- North Texas Police Chiefs Association
- Texas Commission on Law Enforcement
  Master Peace Officer
  Basic Instructor

Honors
- Chamber Public Service Award
- Supervisor of the Year
- Officer of the Year

Publications and Presentations

- 24 on 2024 – *Women in Policing*

- International Association of Chiefs of Police – *Officer Safety and Wellness Conference*
  Mentoring Programs: The Value of Internal Support and How to Start Your Own

- *Incorporating Restorative Justice*

Jane Doe

Ft. Worth, TX • 817-555-5555 • applicant@email.net

Date

Contact Name OR Hiring Manager
Title
Company Name
Address
City, State, Zip

Dear Mr. or Ms. (Contact's Last Name): or Dear Hiring Manager:

It is with great professional enthusiasm that I approach (Company Name) with the goal of exploring available opportunities, such as the (Job Title) opening posted at (site). Equipped with more than 20 years of experience, I am well-prepared to align my skill set and expertise with this position.

My resume is enclosed for your review; highlights include:

- Ten years of successful service at the rank of Lieutenant.
- Expert at policy review/development and drafting grants to secure departmental funding.
- Efficient issue and conflict resolution skills; expertise in Command Critical incidents.
- Held responsibility for the safety and protection of more than 19,000 residents.

In addition, I possess outstanding time-management skills and work well as a leader in team-driven environments. You will find me to be a highly productive individual, quick to grasp essential procedures and protocols, and possessing the expertise to do whatever it takes to complete the task set before me.

Should these characteristics, my diverse experience and my solid work ethic be a good fit with your company, I would look forward to an opportunity to discuss my qualifications in detail. Until then, thank you for your time and consideration.

Sincerely,

Jane Doe

EMPLOYMENT AGREEMENT –EXAMPLE 1

SHORT FORM (FIXED TERM)

This Employment Agreement ("Agreement") is made this 4th day of September, 2025, by and between the **Town of Anywhere** ("Town") and **James R. Doe** ("Chief" or "Employee").

1. Position

The Town hereby employs James R. Doe as **Chief of Police**. The Chief shall perform all duties of the office as prescribed by law, ordinance, and the directives of the Town Manager.

2. Term

This Agreement shall be effective beginning **October 1, 2025**, and shall continue for a period of **two (2) years**, unless earlier terminated as provided herein.

3. Compensation

The Chief shall receive an annual salary of **$125,000**, payable according to the Town's payroll schedule. Salary adjustments may be considered annually by the Town Council.

4. Benefits

The Chief shall be entitled to all benefits afforded to department directors, including health insurance, retirement, vacation leave, sick leave, and use of a Town-issued vehicle for official purposes.

5. Termination

- **Without Cause:** Either party may terminate this Agreement with **60 days' written notice**. If terminated by the Town without cause, the Chief shall receive a severance payment equal to **three (3) months of base salary**.
- **For Cause:** The Town may terminate this Agreement immediately for cause, including misconduct, violation of law, or neglect of duty.

6. Entire Agreement

This document represents the full agreement between the parties and may be amended only in writing, signed by both parties.

IN WITNESS WHEREOF, the parties have executed this Agreement as of the date written above.

James R. Doe, Chief of Police

Karen L. Smith, Town Manager – Town of Anywhere

EMPLOYMENT AGREEMENT – EXAMPLE 2

Chief of Police Employment Agreement

This Employment Agreement ("Agreement") is made and entered into this 4th day of September, 2025, by and between the **City of Anytown, a municipal corporation** ("City"), and **Jane A. Doe** ("Chief" or "Employee").

1. Position and Duties

The City hereby employs Jane A. Doe as **Chief of Police** of the Anytown Police Department. The Chief shall have full responsibility for the management, administration, and operation of the department, subject to the policies of the City Council and the direction of the City Manager.

2. Term of Employment

This Agreement shall commence on **October 1, 2025**, and continue for a term of **three (3) years**, unless earlier terminated in accordance with this Agreement.

3. Compensation

The City shall pay the Chief an annual salary of **$135,000**, payable in accordance with the City's payroll practices. The City agrees to review the Chief's salary annually and may adjust compensation at its discretion.

4. Benefits

The Chief shall be entitled to all benefits generally available to department heads, including health insurance, retirement contributions, vacation leave, sick leave, and use of a City-owned vehicle for official duties.

5. Performance Evaluation

The City Manager shall conduct an annual written performance evaluation of the Chief, providing an opportunity for feedback and discussion of goals.

6. Termination

- **Without Cause:** Either party may terminate this Agreement with **60 days' written notice**. If terminated without cause, the Chief shall be entitled to a severance payment equal to **six (6) months of base salary**.
- **For Cause:** The City may terminate the Chief immediately for cause, including but not limited to misconduct, violation of law, or substantial neglect of duties.

7. Entire Agreement

This document constitutes the entire agreement between the parties and supersedes any prior agreements or understandings.

IN WITNESS WHEREOF, the parties have executed this Agreement as of the date first above written.

Jane A. Doe, Chief of Police

Mary Johnson, City Manager – City of Anytown

EMPLOYMENT AGREEMENT – EXAMPLE 3

Chief of Police Employment Agreement

This Agreement is entered into as of September 4, 2025, by and between the **Town of Fairview** ("Town") and **Jane Doe** ("Chief" or "Employee").

1. Appointment and Duties

The Town agrees to employ Jane Doe as **Chief of Police**. The Chief shall perform all duties as prescribed by state law, municipal ordinances, and the policies of the Town Council.

2. Term

This Agreement shall be effective beginning **September 15, 2025**, and shall remain in effect for **two (2) years**, unless extended or terminated as provided herein.

3. Compensation

The Chief shall receive an annual salary of **$120,000**, payable in accordance with the Town's payroll schedule. Salary adjustments may be considered annually during the budget process.

4. Benefits and Perquisites

The Chief shall be entitled to:

- Participation in the Town's health, dental, and retirement plans;
- **Twenty (20) vacation days** annually, in addition to standard holidays;
- Use of a **Town-issued vehicle** for business and reasonable personal use;

- Professional development, including training, seminars, and membership dues for professional associations, as approved by the Town Manager.

5. Performance Review

The Town Manager shall evaluate the Chief's performance no less than once per year and provide written feedback.

6. Termination

- **By Town:** The Town may terminate this Agreement at any time with **90 days' written notice**. If terminated without cause, the Chief shall receive a severance package equal to **four (4) months' salary**.
- **By Chief:** The Chief may resign at any time by giving the Town at least **60 days' notice**.
- **For Cause:** Termination may be immediate if the Chief engages in gross misconduct, insubordination, or criminal activity.

7. Governing Law

This Agreement shall be governed by and construed under the laws of the State.

IN AGREEMENT WHEREOF, the parties execute this Agreement as of the date written above.

Jane Doe, Chief of Police

Mary Johnson, Town Manager – Town of Anytown

[i] Local Police Departments Personnel, Bureau of Justice Statistics. https://bjs.ojp.gov/media/68016/download0

[ii] Law Enforcement Management Institute of Texas (2025)

[iii] Todak (2023). "A panel of good ol' boys": Women navigating the police promotions process. American Journal of Criminal Justice, 48 (4) 967 – 983.

Made in the USA
Coppell, TX
18 February 2026

72324524R00075